CLOSE READING

FLOYD
SKLOOT

CLOSE READING

EYEWEAR PUBLISHING

First published in 2014
by Eyewear Publishing Ltd
74 Leith Mansions, Grantully Road
London w9 1lj
United Kingdom

Typeset with graphic design by Edwin Smet
Author photograph Beverly Hallberg
Printed in England by TJ International Ltd, Padstow, Cornwall

ISBN 978-1-908998-19-4

WWW.EYEWEARPUBLISHING.COM

For Beverly with love

and

Ron Slate with gratitude
for forty years of friendship

Floyd Skloot's poetry, memoirs, essays, and fiction
have won three Pushcart Prizes, the PEN USA Literary Award,
two Pacific Northwest Book Awards, and been finalists for the
Barnes & Noble Discover Award, the PEN Award for the Art of
the Essay, and the Paterson Prize in Poetry. In 2010, he was named
by Poets & Writers Inc. as "one of fifty of the most inspiring authors
in the world." His work has appeared in *The Best American Essays*,
Best American Science Writing, *Best Spiritual Writing*, and *Best Food
Writing*. Skloot's most recent books include the poetry collections
The Snow's Music and *The End of Dreams* (both from Louisiana
State University Press, 2006 and 2008), and *Revertigo: An
Off-Kilter Memoir* (University of Wisconsin Press, 2014).
Skloot is the father of the bestselling writer Rebecca Skloot,
author of *The Immortal Life of Henrietta Lacks*.
He lives in Portland, OR, with his wife,
Beverly Hallberg.

Table of Contents

I

THE PROMISE OF LIGHT

John Donne in London, December 1623

Confined to bed by spotted fever,
Donne thinks clearly but feels
himself adrift between this world
and the next. The bells calling
their oldest daughter to the altar
are also his late wife's voice
calling across the last threshold.
They drown the fading echoes
of a summons to prayer he heard
somewhere to the south. The air
is dark with cold, but he burns
as he looks through the open
window at a sudden burst of light,
surely the bride's radiant smile
he has yearned for years to see.
So it is finished, as he wished,
and he is released now to live
or die as God sees fit. This is
the time to give thanks. But then
his fever spikes, seizing his breath
for the moment it takes sleep
to drift down like a sheet
of paper he knows he must fill.

Pachelbel in Nuremberg, Winter 1706

The first dream is a windswept hillside
he has never seen, somewhere in Spain
where he has never been. He stands
there facing the sea as a second dream
enters the scene, and he is also in a field
of Swiss wildflowers. No, he is a wildflower,
purple gentian, and his delicate head swirls
as a third dream lifts him above Nuremberg
while leaving him both in the radiant field
and upon the desolate hillside. He wakes
knowing it was all scored to the first moments
of his *Canon in D*, though the only sound
he heard was the howling of heaven.
It has been like this since the year began.

He believes such dreams mean his final
sleep is drawing near, and so has begun
rising at false dawn to walk the streets
alone. His mind is clearest then, the early
winter air filling his shrunken chest again
with youthful breath. His children hear
him leave, but he feels this is good
practice for them all. His heavy step
yields to the night's softening silence,
and he is drawn east toward the promise
of light, the one place melody remains
alive for him. But first he must stop
before his church's great walls to wonder
if all the music he has made there
will remain like a dream in its air.

Thomas Cole at the Kaaterskill Clove, 1825

From the valley floor he looks back
at storm clouds crossing the mountain crest.
Unleashed light moves like the finger of God
over crimson and gold leaves, sandstone shelf,
shale, each tier of the brightening falls.

Watching the pool froth as splashback
smashes against rock, he feels himself close
to all he has sought and feared for years.
There is a voice within the colour and light
deafening him now as he tries to turn away,
to shut his eyes and hold it all still.
Already he imagines quick strokes
of his brush to capture the shock of sky.

He believes what is being revealed to him
about the world he sees is not about the world
he sees. He stares up at the quiet brink
where he knows someone should be standing
on a lustrous boulder, a fellow witness,
then at the seething pool where water readies
itself for another plunge, and at the calmer white
below. It is time for him to continue his journey.
But he cannot bring himself to leave the place
until he sees the entire Clove filled with light.

Jules Verne Above Amiens, 1873

All night Verne visits the balloon
in his mind. Sleep is a dream lost
within the long dream of flight soon
to be real, and time stands still
within the moon-drenched room,
within the envelope of bedsheet
now grown too heavy to be tossed
aside. After all these years! He tries
to forget the balloon is out there,
tethered to the ground in the square
he can almost see in shadows beside
his house. Yearning to rise, teased
by the midnight summer breeze,
waiting for the light of dawn to flare.

*

At first there is too much to see
and feel as he drifts above trees
reddened in the first autumn chill.
He shivers and wonders why
he failed to consider how the soul
might vibrate in such pure air.

The gondola sways when he moves
to follow the Somme bending south,
turns back to catch sunlight flash
off the cathedral dome, leans out
to watch a small boat nudge its way
through marsh, the morning train
shrink as it speeds toward Paris.

He tries to think about issues of lift
and ballast, heat and current, forces
himself to gaze at the barometer
and note its fall. If his calculations
are correct, the sea will soon be
a glimmer in the west. Ambient air
weighs more than... But he finds
himself laughing at the sight of birds
scattering as he passes among them.
Looking up, he sees thin clouds
ripple like an echo of the wind.

★

What he had written of flight before
was drawn from imagination fired
by long study. The extraordinary
voyages of a boy longing for the sea,
polar ice, a glimpse into the earth's
molten core. Of course the whole
fabric of his fiction is thin as the skin
now holding him aloft, but it fills him
with pleasure to feel in his body
how much he has gotten right.

He must take notes. *Transported*
to a world of dreams. He knows
the air is not quite a slow river
but yet he soars as hidden currents
shift, and almost loses his grip.
How could a man not see before
he dies what it is to be free
of the land, to live even for an hour

where his kind cannot live?
Oh, and the sudden uplift is just
as he described it, remembering
his first moments on the water
as a child. With the sun behind him,
Verne looks down into the heart
of Amiens, searching for his home.

Cézanne at Sixty-one

From restless sleep he woke to the same dark
that stained his dreams. He always knew a tint
of midnight dominated the Lord's stark
palette. It was what gave a star's furtive glint
the jolt others saw as hope but he knew
for what it was: a trick air plays on light.
Darkness was the cold, secret core of faith
he had lost long before reaching the age
of sixty-one. But he rose against night's
hold, crossed the meager room. It was still true
that he loved to catch the onrushing sea
as a burst of colour felt in the cones
and rods of his eyes. He still longed to be
where dawn's flares fractured a mountain's bones.

Robert Frost in Old Age

So now he knows the heart remembers loss
the way the woods remember winter storms.
Deadfall litters the trail he follows, forms
a frail, jagged bridge he uses to cross
the surging runoff stream, plays host to swarms
of insects massing as the weather warms,
fills the drenched air with scents of rot and growth.
He walks for the ragged muscle and strained
breath in his chest, for all he can recall
of old griefs and other early Aprils
when he thought the worst was over, the stained
soul cleansed, the way through straight and clear as truth.

Paul Klee at Sixty

Slowly the stillness comes upon his hand.
As he watches, colour bleeds from the tip
of his brush, leaving him only a thick
black line. He has dreamt it time and again
but this is no dream. He knows he is sick
beyond all imagining now. A land
of loss looms, and is the place he must walk
this tired line, which thins as it wavers
toward the vanishing point. He cannot rest.
As his skin shrinks, as his muscles soften,
what he most wants to bring to life is death
as it looks to him here, pure fire often
blazing in the coldest place. He savors
it as he waits for movement to begin.

Robert Louis Stevenson in Samoa, Summer 1894

He is up and about, a small wonder
in itself, savoring the heavy scent
of early September sea air. Under
a tropical sun that has always meant
hope to him, he feels the sort of power
long forgotten in his muscles and bones.
He will work well again after all, hour
by hour in the hot flow of all he knows
about young love on the land of his youth.
The memory of hard winds sends a chill
through him. No, his fever is back, truth
in the form of a wracking cough. He will
sit a moment and listen to the stream
say nothing is ever the way it seems.

Fauré in Paris, 1924

Nearing eighty, Fauré has found the end
of sound. He never would have guessed
it had so much to do with the Mediterranean
light of childhood, or lake breezes swirling
all summer at Savoy, and so little to do
with music growing quieter everywhere
but in his mind. He is relieved to hear
the garbled edge of what had been music,
his torment for twenty years, fading at last
to silence. If only his breath would follow!

He believes he is finished with the flesh,
his face now thin and delicate as a lost note
dissolving in air, his body closing in
on itself, the discordant coda to a life
of elegance and song. He would become
spirit instead, simple and radiant at the level
of pure grace, diaphanous against nightfall.
He hoards his bare, inner music and must
force himself to reduce it to notes on a page.

Alone, deaf to street noise below, the call
of birds above, seeing the Paris sky glazed
with loud sunlight, he feels wrapped
in melody's softest shroud. It is exquisite,
as he always knew it must be, and almost
liquid in the way it lifts him toward the clouds.

II

THE VANISHING POINT

The Shared Room

My brother was a Brylcreemed pompadour
and my brother was rock 'n' roll first thing
every morning. Then he was a four-door
Valiant, smouldering Kent, star-sapphire ring
on the pinky. He was small savvy smiles
and a wink, a deck of cards, shiny suit,
shot cuffs, Windsor knots. My brother was miles
ahead. He was goodbye, a man en route.
I was another story. I was crew
cut and tucked shirt, double-knotted shoes, please
and thank you. I was too small to hit, too
big for my britches. Cracker Barrel cheese
instead of Velveeta. *Sorry*, not *Clue*.
Cute, not suave, and too dumb to be believed.

The Evening Meal

– Brooklyn, 1954

My butcher father brought home a smell
of fowl that no amount of Old Spice,
Lava soap, or cigar smoke could disguise.
Some nights his raspy skin was flecked
with blood. Chicken feathers stuck to the back
of his neck were set aflutter when the door
closed behind him. Though he washed before
dinner, the market was with us as he sat
at the table, knife in hand. I watched his face
flicker through vapours from the dinner platter,
heard breath pass the bones of his broken nose,
and waited. There might be a sigh, lowered brows,
a smile, and then the smell would not matter
anymore, might even vanish without a trace.

Nostrand Avenue

– Brooklyn, 1955

I remember the street was full of noise,
trolleys screeching and sizzling under
sparking wires, taxis honking as braying boys
dashed past and cellar doors thundered shut.
It was autumn and I wanted to hear leaves fall.
My mother's words were air and cigarette
smoke rising toward the clear sky. A bus
gushed to a stop and there were more people
before us, forcing us to stop. I saw a man
dance and flap around the corner to find
a woman holding out her hands to join him.
They whirled, blinded to everything around them
as they laughed and cried. People leaned to cheer
from cars, doorways, windows, rooftops.
A butcher waved his cleaver. A priest wept.
Then a flash of sunlight off a windshield,
and the brush of my mother's overcoat
as she pulled me into the ordinary afternoon
light, fading now like the last note of a song.
No matter how hard I try, this is always
where the memory stops, before I come to
understand the Dodgers have won at last.

New Mitt

– Brooklyn, 1956

At nine I knew exactly what to do:
spread newspaper on floor; gather my
brother's jar of neatsfoot oil, oldest belt,
and battered hardball; find scrap of shoe
polish rag. Play stack of records by
Elvis Presley. Air must be cool and dry.
The honey-coloured leather looked and smelled
like summer but had to turn winter dark
from my touch. The palm blackened and flexed
as I worked oil deep and lost myself
in the ceremony, loving the stark
simplicity of dressing my new mitt
as my brother had dressed his. I sang
along with 'Heartbreak Hotel.' With my fist
I pounded and shaped the fresh pocket,
cinched the ball in tight, then put it in our closet
to season beside his until early spring.

Winter on the Island

– Long Beach, NY, 1959

In late December nothing could keep us
from walking the shoreline to land's end.
Storm by storm we saw high summer sands
flattening until the old year died in a surge
of surf. By then swash stained the beach
grey as the place where sky and rising sea
came together. This was the turning world
as far as we knew it, children learning faith
in longshore drift, the quiet work of currents
beneath all that dark churn and spume.

My Grandparents' Dance

My grandparents' stately polka was done
in waltz time no matter the music's speed.
They turned slow whistling circles that spun
through other dancers' wakes and freed
something in them I had never seen before.
This smiling man was the old-country Max,
so graceful as he moved across the floor
with a hand spread low on Rose's back,
and this gliding woman with fingertips
grazing Max's shoulder flowed on the rise
and fall of their dance as she slipped
the weight of all her years, head back, eyes
closed. Her gown sparkled as she twirled under
his raised arm and he gazed down in wonder.

The Shore

The old men belching up their lunches
take hard rolls from coat pockets,
sit on boardwalk benches, and sigh.
They toss scraps to circling seagulls,
sparing no words for the tumbling surf,
having nothing to say about sunlight
streaming through a break in clouds
right above their heads. It is enough
to frown at one another, brows raised,
and flutter their fingers, which means
don't worry, things will get worse soon,
because by now they all know this God.
So they kvetch about the nursing home's
soups, cream of kohlrabi, cream of carrot,
cream of beet. Enough with the roots,
already! And corn on the cob when no
one has real teeth, chicken cooked since
the end of World War II, crumbling rolls
even a bird spits out. They nearly smile,
warming up, coughing into their hands.
Never such food, not in the old country
when crops failed, not all those winter
months in the woods, or in the hospital
with the gall bladder. Now they nod
and fall silent. My grandfather, sinking
toward sleep, lets the last crumbs scatter.

Wet Light

After five days of autumn rain
and early nights

the wind-rippled surface
of this empty street

glimmering as clouds part
for a moment

has become the wake
of a ferry

I remember from childhood
the shimmer

of wet light on the deck
as we crossed

the river toward home
my father

with his arm holding
me still

and dwindling into the dark
distance another

ferry with its wake now
meeting ours.

The Lost Language

My mother spoke
the lost language of storm
native to the island
of her shattered mind.
It had an endless swarm
of words for *rage*
but one for *love*,
which was the same as *cage*,
and in the least shift
of tone I could find
a hundred meanings
for the verb *to warn*.
Her silence had
a syntax of its own.
I read it clearly
now that she is gone.

Lullaby

The last time I saw my mother
she was turned toward the wall
with her eyes closed. Light fell
across her body and flickered
as a spring wind passed through
leaves outside her open window.
Breath shallow, lips sealed, still
she held onto life as I began
singing to her, squeezing between
bed and wall so she could feel
the familiar words drift over her.
Halfway through the final verse
her eyes suddenly opened wide.
They moved across my face,
across the space between us,
then vanished from sight as she
returned to sleep. The song ended,
and I knew it was time for silence.

My Brother Waits

My brother waits for me in a room long gone,
in a building restored to the rubble of its lot,
on a city block zoned now for lost memories.
He waits for me where time has ceased
to matter, where his breath, stilled so long,
flows as light across my face in the space
we once shared. He is far away, close
to the vanishing point but coming clear,
waiting for me, blind eyes full of summer
dazzle, laughter like froth on a distant wave.

The Race

A gunshot echoes in the dream's still air.
Swallows scatter, then gather again
to become my father cresting a hill
as I begin to run, seeing nothing but light
where he is headed. I keep him within
my heart and mind until the distance
between us closes, and he is back
in sight. I slow to a trot, then stop
but still gain ground. The sound
of his ragged breath before me exposes
how near we are now to the end.

Almost Equinox

– for my daughter on her 35th birthday

I remember the night you were born was warm
and calm after the daylong forecast of storms.
It was almost equinox. I must have heard Elvis
sing 'Burning Love' ten times that day, stuck
in traffic going to work and again coming home,
turning off the news of letter bombs and napalm.
For dinner we ate Mexican food, and mistook
the first labor pains for heartburn. Of the quick
drive to the hospital what I remember most is
moonlit silence, a clear space ahead where
I saw the skein of chance bringing us together
was more delicate than a hummingbird's feather.

III

A PRIMARY APPRECIATION

Close Reading

– for Thomas Kinsella

The sun sank behind us as we drove past
Crab Orchard Lake in my battered Falcon.
It coughed and rattled at forty but we spoke
above the noise, three young poets eager
for our evening's close reading with the master.
'Fern Hill' was about the lost childhood Eden!
'Fern Hill' was about death! About time!
All poems were about Death and Time!

In his formal dining room, Kinsella placed
us at the table like poker players beneath
a blazing chandelier. We spread the text
and bent to our task. Then he asked why
the poem began with *Now* and brought
all pronouncements to a sudden stop.

★

Gerry sat in an oak rocker, dangling one
last ornament for his Christmas tree.
Bob and I stood across the small room,
ready with advice. The doorbell rang.
Kinsella entered, gloved, hatted, stamping
snow from his boots, streaming vapor
as he spoke, helping Eleanor remove
her coat. We shook his hand and asked
where he thought the ornament should go.

He studied Gerry's tree, blinked at its blinking
lights, said things were perfect as they were:
Anything more would just be for effect.

★

At forty-one he seemed correct and neat
as a sonnet. The thick beard trimmed, hair flat
across his scalp, voice clear, words precise, feet
on the floor like a couplet when he sat.
But there was something radical going
on beneath the surface. Order opposed
by sheer formlessness in new work growing
stranger as he turned inward. I supposed
he would teach me how to write poems clean
and tight as he used to write them, verse strict
as he looked. That he would reveal to me
the secret of where poems came from. He
would show me the hidden ways to inflict
form, and what being a poet might mean.

★

Instead, we practiced close reading.
Who is speaking in the second stanza?
We scoured excess, awkward statement,
clotted imagery, extreme verbal gesture,
slackness, the least readiness to settle
for the rhetorical. *See here, a bee
cannot repeatedly sting. This is false.*
We followed the management of data
in every poem, found the order it sought
to establish. *What's a foot doing here?*

Nothing should stand between the poet
and the thing perceived. *Montague
does not encrust his verse irrelevantly.*

At winter's end, Gerry, Bob, and I stopped
to buy a fifth of Jameson and handed it
to Kinsella when he opened the door.
He read the label, almost smiled, and set
the bottle down on a credenza. Saying
we'll address this later, he led us to
the dining table where the light never wavered.

★

Our poems were read in the living room,
not the dining room. We sat in a loose
arc of easy chairs, subjecting the work
to *a primary appreciation*. One night
a month to us, three nights to Eliot,
Pound, Murphy. He would call one
of our names, nod in the chosen poet's
direction, lift the paper into the light
of his reading lamp, and direct
his avid glance to our words.

★

At seventy-nine, his voice on the disc
is still deep and direct. He reads his work
as you would expect, the tone sharp, pace brisk.
Nothing wasted, no frills. If shadows lurk,
they lurk where they should, in the poems' dark
depths brought to light by his words. I will hear

this voice to the end of my days, the stark
truth of it over time, helping me clear
my own way toward what I need to say.

Isaac Bashevis Singer in the Reading Room, 1968

This old man in the armchair's plush embrace
waits for his thoughts to settle. He is not
my grandfather despite the wrinkled face,
gleaming skull, vast snout, gargly voice, and odd
twist of lips. They sound like men from the same
village in an old country bordering
on nowhere to be found again. He takes
a deep breath and shifts his weight, ordering
familiar words he has brought together
to address the final question of the night:
You see, I'm only a storyteller,
not a psychologiser. I just write
a beginning, a middle, and an end.
The meaning I leave to you, my good friend.

In Thompson Woods with John Gardner, 1970

He shuffled through my poems as we walked
along the trail. Falling hickory leaves grazed
his hair. He slapped the pages when he talked.
"Never use the word *tremble*." The path, glazed
with morning rain, crossed a patch of sunlight
and his face turned a moment toward the sky.
"Don't use *awe*, either, but feel it." To our right
as the wind rose, oak limbs bowed in a shy
curtsy. "And call things by their proper names."
He stopped to light his pipe and explain why
everyone should write at least one epic,
as he was doing, because the lyric
was a romantic trap. He closed one eye.
"Remember, art's not just fun and games."

The Reading

– for Stanley Kunitz

The poet was old, the age I am now,
and he swayed like the ancient Jews
I prayed with as a child. What I knew
of his work was stiff with study, slow
to open itself. But this was all new,
clear, a psalm felt in his sinews.
I saw that he smiled as he moved
and was moved, the poem still true
for him in the moment he spoke
it. Something found like a stone
in a ditch, discovered out of the blue
as he walked the usual way home.

Miranda at Midnight

"Be not afeard, the isle is full of noises."
– William Shakespeare, *The Tempest*

Magic lets me see her in the dim light
of a new moon. I remember that smile
lingering in the young woman's midnight
face, a child's trace of wonder at the wild
familiar twangling that is all she knows
of sea winds across the same stunted trees,
rocks, coves, caves. Now the island's voice grows
softer even as it rises, and sleep
is what it sings. I can see what she sees
in this still moment before time resumes,
hear what she hears, through our dreams' sorceries.
Again and again day's first light consumes
these riches, and at night I seize them back.
But in the island's noise I hear the beat
of my own heart at last. No more magic,
it says. Let her go. There is nothing to fear.

Thomas Hardy in Oregon, Summer 2007

Dawn sun glints off the dome
of a golden statue I never saw
in our garden before.
Not squat,
like my wife's stone Buddha
snug in its niche on the gazebo,
but taut
with a kind of waking energy,
and life-size for a man of my own height.
A breeze tosses the lilac's leaves
until shadows crossing the figure's skull
make it seem to blink.
An arm rises as though to clear
away a spider's web.

I know it must be the extra midnight
dose of Chinese herbs lingering
in my system,
combined
with the way first light runs wild below.
I know
it is a trick of muddled perception.
But then the statue speaks,
scattering a cluster of crows
that gathers every morning at the fence line,
and turns tearful eyes
toward the place where they have flown.
All's past amend, unchangeable.

This is the face of the aged
                    Hardy,
            with a wisp of cloud
above his wrinkled brow, the darting
            glance attuned to loss
    and wary of any change,
the moustache rhyming with thin downturned lips.
                He wants a bare,
            wind-driven landscape
                    known to the depths of his soul
but finds himself in our lush profusion
                    of glory
    bower, hollyhocks, coneflower,
            rock rose, chaste tree, lavender,
everything in bloom and nothing native
    to his startled, worried sight.

    I have been reading him again.
            Just last month, the flawed
                    romances
                of his middle years,
last week the familiar elegies for Emma,
    their faded passion flaming up
                    only
    in the wake of her sudden death.
        Perhaps the grief that set him
            wandering after her
                    keeps him
            adrift in time and space now.
    He looks worn by more than years
            and grief as the wind swirls.

Glancing into the dark
beyond me,
he finds what he came here for
and so do I. Once more
his arm lifts, a wave this time,
equal parts farewell and blessing.
So I move back to bed,
where my wife stirs in her sleep,
calling my name,
and I know we will soon be whispering
the strange
story of our night's dreamings.

At Rowan Oak

– Oxford, Mississippi

Faulkner is nowhere and everywhere
here, adrift among oak grown thick
with all the years he has been gone.
Scent of magnolia sweetens the air.
Shadows litter the portico as we walk
the alley of cedars. Summer heat rises
to shimmer between us and the white
clapboard home that keeps him still
for us in time. Inside, an office wall
is covered with the outline of *A Fable*.
A small table holds his old Underwood.
My daughter, freshly finished writing
her first book, leans across the threshold.

IV

VERTIGO

Last Winter

An innocent cough, vague pain in the joints
when he plays simple chords, muted rashes
across his torso, sudden sundown flashes
of fever. His dreams know. Everything points
to relapse though he thought there would be
more time, though his doctors said the signs
were all good. Now and then there are times
when he can still dissemble, when the tree
outside his window suddenly resumes its shape
against the backdrop of his neighbor's fence,
when the light lingers long enough to convince
him winter has lost its way. When he can escape
what he feels happening in his body's core
where nothing like it had reached before.

Terminal Condition

He feels his battle is not with cancer
or chemo but with health insurance claims.
There seems no way to get a straight answer
in time. It is like reading Henry James,

sentences turning upon themselves, all
delay and denial, leading nowhere
he has the time to go. Another call,
another hour on hold. This is health care

in America, a system as sick
as his own, devoured by growth gone wild,
destroying what it is meant to sustain.
Now a new voice is trying to explain
the problem with treatment codes in his file
as, on the desk nearby, an old clock ticks.

The Lost Hour

Time did not stop. I remember talking
with the young doctor about his New York
years, then my clean bowels, and he was walking
away, a nurse swabbing where veins fork
in my hand, my wife leaning over to kiss
my lips, my daughter's voice on the cell
phone laughing. No sense of a moment missed,
an hour gone, only knowing all was well
where before there was concern, since time
could be catching up to me – a man
of sixty – in the form of secret growth,
past appetites, or an inheritance both
latent and malign. But they all say I'm
safe for now, should rise again when I can.

The Onset of Vertigo

I woke one morning to a whirling world.
The room spun counterclockwise, taking me
down with it. On all fours, I watched
the door jamb sway and thought *earthquake*.
But the floor was still and the walls held
together. So this was going on inside
my head. I spoke to see if I could,
blinked to see if that changed the way
I saw things, moved fingers and toes,
rocked back on my naked haunches.
My head didn't hurt. I knew where I was
in the world and time. My wife stirred
behind me in bed. I tried to calm myself:
over sixty, rose too quickly, wax in ears,
sudden change of weather in the early
spring. A dream. Nothing to worry about.
Nothing to say it would last six months.
I would stand if I could get a grip on
something more solid than undulating air.

Sway

I lie back on the narrow bed
and do not know what to do
with my hands. A woman
looms above me, fitting two
chocks tight against my head,
and warns me yet again
not to move. Earphones hiss.
I close my eyes before
beginning to slip
into the magnet's bore.
Soon I hear faint music play
beneath the MRI's
jackhammer rattle. 'Sway,'
by Dean Martin, and I
feel its mambo rhythm take
hold down through my toes.
It is all I can do to make
them be still as Dino's
soused-sounding baritone
fills my brain. I need to sing
along now. I have known
this song, from the first *bing*
bing of the chorus to the last
mellow *now*, since learning
the lyrics as a boy whose vast
fantasies included turning
himself into a crooner. I am
in a bath of sense, memory,
and dye. My brain scan
must be lit up like a night sky

by the Northern Lights. But no,
it is not that kind of test,
and then the music stops so
I can hear that the next
phase will last fifteen
minutes, that I have done
very well so far, and please
remember to be still again.

Vincent Van Gogh, Self Portrait

> "I suffer from vertigo"
> – Vincent Van Gogh, 1888

I recognize the look: neck tucked and still,
shoulders hunched, back rounded into a shell,
and the eyes held level as the world swirls
around him. Clouds wheel above cypresses
and wheat fields, hills and spires, everywhere
he turns. Saint-Rémy, Arles, the very air
of Auvers is a seething vortex. Even his room
lists, as mine does now though I am still,
though I hold my eyes level against the whorls
and loops of walls turning liquid everywhere
I look. Sometimes Van Gogh himself presses
by me on the stairs, hisses *this is hell*
when we stumble together. Or I see
his reflection flicker across windowpanes,
his face reveal itself when lilacs dance
in the garden, his form in the fluky space
where shadows flicker. I recognize his light
rippling like visible current under the sea
of night sky. Watch him paint through dazed pain
the turbulence of an olive orchard in space
crazed by kinesis. Go with him after light
spinning toward us in its quickening dance.

Mr. Equilibrium & Mr. Vertigo

Moonlight finds me balanced on a strand
of spider's silk as I cross a gorge.
Below, invisible currents roar
and roil the air but I am steady,
a man out for a stroll. And why not
pirouette as wind turns wild since I
am impervious to dizziness?
I can do away with light and line,
become *Mr. Equilibrium*
poised on sheer air above the abyss.
But then at the moment of waking
I recognize a familiar face.
Mr. Vertigo, still playing tricks,
leers at me from the horizon's edge.

Standup Routine

Did you hear the one about the man
who goes on a Caribbean cruise
and after four days at sea his brain
never again knows when he's on land?
Dizzy forever, a joke among nerves,
eyes, skin, ankles and inner ear
whispering and tittering in private.

I heard it from the famous balance
specialist who warned me not to step
foot on a boat now that vertigo has
me in its hold. Why he thought I might
even consider boating is beyond me,
since seeing leaves move in a breeze
is enough to make me swoon
and the least turning of my head
makes me reel. But okay, no boats.

Also, without being told, no bicycles,
sambas, Ferris wheels, ladders, swan
dives. Very little looking at skies,
especially with clouds in motion,
and no imagining flocks of starlings
as they turn in unison because just
the thought of that makes me queasy.
Best to plan, calculate each movement,
hold myself still to match the stillness
of an Earth that never stops moving.

How about the one where the man
lives like that for half a year,
and one night while reading beside
his wife on the couch feels the entire
inside of his head expand until
he can't hear a thing, then contract
in one heartbeat? I stand up and am
no longer dizzy, so I go to the window
and look out at the cloud-crossed moon.
I'm still standing after imagining kayaks
and carnival rides, so I think it's time
to turn around and ask my wife to dance.

V

DUSK AT THE EDGE
OF THE WORLD

Painted Lady

My wife stands among the drumstick
allium at her garden's eastern border.
Camera poised in late afternoon light,
she waits as a painted lady circles,
lands on the deep scarlet flower,
then flies off when a honeybee climbs
beside it like a weary mountaineer.
No breeze, no clouds, and now I see
I am not even breathing as she holds
still, watching, whispering to the air.
The butterfly returns, comes to rest,
and slowly opens its brilliant wings.

Summer Solstice

Above Eagle Crest the day's first
breaths were wisps of cirrus
curling across a quarter moon.
Scents of rose and lavender
drifted through the open window
as though let loose by the mourning
doves' notes. It was too hot
too soon for this early in the year,
a dawn that seemed to warn
as much as welcome. Behind me
I heard my wife shift and sigh
in the grip of her dream, wiser
even in sleep to time's sure turnings.

End of July

The sliver of new moon is a skiff
rocking on heat and haze.
Such motion has a tune
whippoorwills, loons, and great
horned owls know, but tonight
hold fast. So time does not dance.
Air stops its breath. Light folds
over itself like a wave
and breaks beyond the horizon.

Looking Back

That morning my wife and I felt
summer lose its grip. Nothing more
than a waning of the scents that dwelt
all season near the hilltop, or
softer light, an edge to the breeze
we were not even sure was there.
It was still too early for leaves
to change colour, though we saw where
that would begin as we looked back
into the sunlit grove of oak.
When we continued our slow walk
to the crest, neither of us spoke.

Blank Journal

On Memorial Day, 1992,
I bought this journal whose pages remain
blank except for the date and coffee-stained
flyleaf. Tucked between pages one and two,
the receipt tells me exactly where I stood
when I first knew I was in love with you:
corner of Fourth and Taylor, just past noon.
I remember the weather was so good
for late May that I walked to the river
and kept hearing the phrase *I'll see her soon*
like a song playing over and over
in my mind. What a perfect first entry
for the new journal, I thought. But instead
of going back to buy an emergency
pen at the store, I turned toward home, my head
filled with the melody of seeing you soon.

Early Winter

As we drove west out of the city
each turn took us deeper into the dark
and fog. Each road was narrower
the closer we got to home. The sky
folded down around us. Traffic thinned.

Those were nights when warmth
ruffling through the car like breath
still left us cold. Just beyond Dundee
the road forked south across sunken
tracks where the air was clear
as the dead center of winter.

Then fog waiting at the next bend
swamped us again. We slowed
when a single brilliant light appeared
to float above the road, surging east
through the air as though drawn
toward prey. We could not stop in time,
could barely react before the road
dipped and the roaring train passed
over us on a trestle that came from
nowhere we remembered being before.

Open Country

It is both spring and summer here
where we have stopped, halfway home.
Lupine blues the hillside still capped
in snow, the air braces as it warms
between drifting clouds, and a late
afternoon squall brews to the west.
We walk to the fence and stretch.
Calves bolting from our shadows lose
themselves in the sheer joy of play.
We can almost touch a rippled ridge
of Ponderosa Pine that could be five
miles away. Now the light we saw leave
the tops of those trees flows downslope.
It seems to stagger across a fold of land,
then ripple through the grass on its way
to find us where we stand together.

Abbaye de Sènanque

Two miles north of Gordes the road swooped
into a valley of sunlight and lavender.
As we drove, the abbey's stone walls glowed
deep rose, changed to honey-gold against a grove
of oak, then blanched when we turned to face it.
I imagined sanctuary from the heat, a gentler light,
the peace of stillness after a full week of travel.
I imagined voices lifted in song lifting me out
of myself, the silly irritations of a body and mind
already yearning for home. The air, drenched
in scent, hung like a sheet above the church dome.
I heard a dry drone speak of summer temperatures
gone beyond the reach of shadow or prayer.
When we stopped, the car ticked and dripped.
A man sat at his easel as though stunned,
brush raised, gaze trained at the space
where lavender massed into a shimmering
purple lake. Dozens of people moved past him
to shelter under the trees. We followed in silence,
merging with others returning from the abbey
and shaking their heads. It was closed.
I looked back up at the rocky ridge, its dark
foliage absorbing the direct light. Then I felt
my wife's breath against my neck, her laugh
a whisper breaking softly into song.

Dusk at the Edge of the World

Moonrise softens the lake's steel blue
to sky, and wind-driven ripples to powder.
Those distant shadows are boats docked
near cottages huddled on this narrow spit
at land's end. For a moment, we are deaf
to the ocean beyond, lost in the surrender
of colour that means the world still turns.
The cold, when it comes, is another form
of light. It leads us back toward home.

Closing in July

We planned to live here at least fifteen years,
buying this house to grow old in,
which didn't take as long as we thought.

Built this garden from a weedy yard,
replaced the shake roof, painted outside and in.
We planned to live here at least fifteen years.

She had spaces for music, weaving, art,
and I had a quiet room to write in.
But it didn't take as long as we thought

for her back to give out in the garden,
for my balance to fail on the stairs.
We planned to live here at least fifteen years

but abandoned it room by room. Four years
later it belongs to somebody else.
It didn't take as long as we thought,

and the light feels the same as the day we moved
in, crazed by heat through maple leaves.
We planned to live here a good fifteen years.
It didn't take as long as we thought.

Acknowledgements

These poems appeared in the following journals:

Bellevue Literary Review: 'Looking Back'; *Boulevard*: 'John Donne in London, December 1623' and 'Isaac Bashevis Singer in the Reading Room, 1968'; *Burnside Review Oregon Issue*: 'My Brother Waits'; *The Galway Review* (Ireland): 'My Brother Waits,' 'Paul Klee at Sixty' and 'Painted Lady'; *The Hardy Review:* 'Thomas Hardy in Oregon, Summer 2007'; *The Hopkins Review*: 'Last Winter,' 'Sway,' and 'Terminal Condition'; *The Hudson Review*: 'In Thompson Woods with John Gardner, 1970' and 'Jules Verne Above Amiens, 1873'; *Image*: 'Fauré in Paris, 1924' and 'Thomas Hardy in Oregon, Summer 2007'; *Irish Studies Review* (Ireland): 'Close Reading'; *Margie*: 'The Race' and 'Summer Solstice'; *North American Review*: 'New Mitt'; *Notre Dame Review*: 'End of July,' 'The Onset of Vertigo,' 'The Shared Room,' and 'Thomas Cole at the Kaaterskill Clove, 1825'; *OnEarth*: 'Dusk at the Edge of the World'; *The Pinch*: 'Nostrand Avenue'; *Prairie Schooner*: 'Abbaye de Sènanque,' 'Almost Equinox,' 'Blank Journal,' 'Cézanne at Sixty-one,' 'Close Reading,' 'Closing in July,' 'The Evening Meal,' 'The Lost Hour,' 'Lullaby,' 'Mr. Equilibrium & Mr. Vertigo,' 'The Shore,' 'Standup Routine,' 'Wet Light,' and 'Winter on the Island'; *The Sewanee Review*: 'My Grandparents' Dance,' 'Miranda at Midnight,' 'Paul Klee at Sixty,' 'Robert Frost in Old Age,' and 'Robert Louis Stevenson in Samoa, Summer 1894'; *The SHOp* (Ireland): 'Wet Light'; *The Southern Review*: 'The Lost Language' and 'Pachelbel in Nuremberg, Winter 1706'; *Sou'wester*: 'Early Winter'; *Superstition Review*: 'Open Country'; *Tiferet*: 'Painted Lady'; *TriQuarterly Online*: 'Vincent Van Gogh, Self Portrait'; *Upstairs at Duroc* (France): 'Cézanne at Sixty-one'; *Valparaiso Poetry Review*: 'At Rowan Oak' and 'The Reading'.

ᴗᴗ EYEWEAR PUBLISHING